P9-DDI-148

CACTUS

CACTUS

PETER MURRAY

THE CHILD'S WORLD®

The desert is a hot, dry, unfriendly place to live. Weeks or months go by without a drop of rain. The burning sun bakes the barren soil, driving out every last bit of moisture. Animals travel for miles to find the nearest watering hole.

Plants can't move like animals. Most plants prefer to live in places where there is plenty of water, but some plants have adapted to the dry desert lands.

Desert grasses grow quickly after a rainstorm, produce seeds, and then die. The hardy creosote bush, on the other hand, sends its roots deep into the earth, searching out underground water.

The cactus family has evolved another way to survive in the desert.

Cactus plants have thousands of thin, widespread roots that grow just under the surface of the ground. When it rains, the roots quickly absorb the water. The thick, leafless stem of the cactus stores water like a giant sponge. It swells to hold as much moisture as possible. After a good rain, a cactus can be more than ninety percent water! A waxy coating on the thick, tough skin prevents precious water from evaporating. The cactus uses water slowly—it might have to wait months for the next rainstorm.

What do you say when you run into a cactus?

"Ouch!"

Most cacti are covered by hundreds of sharp spines. It's their way of saying, "Don't mess with me, or you'll be sorry!"

Some cactus spines are long and sharp and stiff. Others are so short and fine you can hardly see them. Fishhook cacti have hook-shaped spines that snag anything that brushes against them. Long ago, people used the spines to catch fish.

Like roses, cacti are prickly to touch yet produce beautiful flowers. Most cacti flower in the spring after the rains have supplied them with plenty of water. The blooms fill the desert with splashes of color. *Cholla cacti* have red, purple, or pink flowers. The tips of the *barrel* cactus and the flat lobes of the *prickly pear* are studded with yellow and orange blossoms. The *night-blooming cereus* looks like a small, uninteresting cactus most of the year, but when its huge, beautiful blossom opens, the air fills with a wonderful perfume.

Cacti are native to North and South America. In the United States, they grow in every state except Alaska, Hawaii, Vermont, New Hampshire, and Maine. Most cacti live in the dry, hot desert regions of the Southwest. The Sonoran Desert, which stretches from Mexico up into Arizona and California, contains thousands of cactus species. The cacti range in size from the thumb-sized *pincushion* cactus to the giant *saguaro*.

Spiny, cactus-like plants called *Euphorbia* grow in Africa and Asia, but they are not related to cacti. True cacti have small, hairy pads on their stems called *areoles*. Spines, flowers, fruits, and new branches begin growing at these areoles.

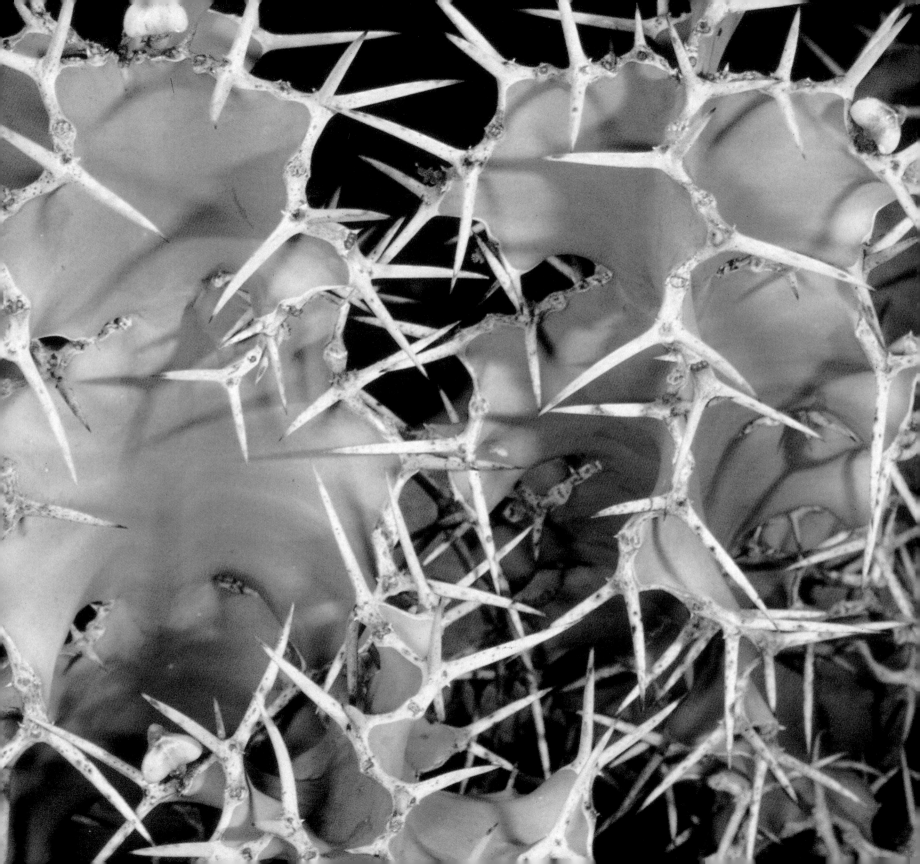

Although the spines and tough skins of cactus plants keep most animals away, a few creatures have learned to use cacti for shelter. The Gila woodpecker makes its nest by pecking holes high in the stems of the giant saguaro cactus. After the woodpecker has nested and moved out, a tiny elf owl might take over its hole. The *jumping cholla* cactus is one of the spiniest cacti in the world, yet the gentle mourning dove builds her nest right in the middle of all those sharp spikes! The cactus spines protect the dove and its offspring from predators.

Cacti also provide food for both animals and people. Every June, the Tohono O'Odham people of the Sonoran Desert harvest the red fruit of the saguaro. They use long poles to pull the fruit from the saguaro's tall branches. The fruit is used to make candy, jam, and sweet drinks. The tasty saguaro fruit also attracts bats, birds, lizards, and other animals.

The saguaro is the largest of all the cacti. A large saguaro can grow up to fifty feet tall—as tall as a four-story building! Some saguaros are over two hundred years old.

The *prickly pear* cactus, named for its pear-shaped fruits, is also a favorite food. People and animals eat the soft, juicy fruits. Sometimes you can find them in grocery stores, where they are called "cactus pears." Hungry cattle eat even the tough, spiny leaves of the prickly pear.

The prickly pear is the most widespread cactus species. It grows from Canada all the way to the tip of South America. When people brought the plant to Australia, the prickly pear grew so quickly that it took over cropland and became a pest plant.

Not all cacti grow in the desert. One common house-plant, the *Christmas cactus*, is native to the rainforests of South America. The Christmas cactus and its relatives live in the treetops, attaching themselves to the trunks of tall trees.

Another group of tropical cacti, the *Pereskia,* are the only cacti that have large leaves. Pereskia plants look like leafy bushes, vines, or small trees. If it weren't for their spines and the small areoles on their stems, you would never know they were in the cactus family.

Although the spiny, thick-skinned cactus might seem like the toughest plant around, it is very sensitive to changes in its environment. Many species can grow only in certain types of soil or certain climates. In the southwestern United States, much of the cactus habitat is being destroyed to make room for roads and buildings, and some rare cactus species are being stolen from their natural habitat by plant collectors.

One out of every four cactus species is now in danger of extinction. Even the mighty saguaro has seen its numbers reduced by pollution and loss of habitat. Fortunately, cacti are now protected by law in many areas. One hundred years from now, this saguaro might stand fifty feet tall!

INDEX

Photo Research
Kristee Flynn

Photo Credits
C. Allen Morgan: cover, 11, 18, 21
Robert & Linda Mitchell: 2, 13, 17, 22, 24, 27
COMSTOCK/Gary Benson: 4, 14, 28
COMSTOCK/J. Oetzel: 7
Jeff Foott: 8
COMSTOCK/Michael Thompson: 31

Library of Congress Cataloging-in-Publication Data
Murray, Peter, 1952 Sept. 29-
Cactus / by Peter Murray.
p. cm.
Includes Index.
ISBN 1-56766-191-2

1. Cactus--Juvenile literature.   [1. Cactus.]   I. Title.
QK495.C11M87   1995   95-5001
583'.47--dc20